Writing in the Ancient World

WRITING IN ANCIENT CHINA

JIL FINE

The Rosen Publishing Group's
PowerKids Press™
New York

Published in 2003 by The Rosen Publishing Group, Inc.
29 East 21st Street, New York, NY 10010

First Edition

Book Design: Michael DeLisio

Photo Credits: Cover, p. 11 © Lowell Georgia/Corbis; p. 4 Arthur M. Sackler Museum, Harvard University/The Bridgeman Art Library; pp. 5, 16, 17 Michael DeLisio; pp. 6–7 Asian Art Museum of San Francisco, The Avery Brundage Collection, Chong-Moon Lee Center For Asian Art and Culture, B60 B1+ and B60 B1 detail; p. 8 © Werner Forman/Art Resource, NY; pp. 9, 10 © Royal Ontario Museum/Corbis; p. 9 (top) British Museum, London/The Bridgeman Art Library; p. 12 © Eye Ubiquitous/Corbis; p. 13 © Dean Conger/Corbis; pp. 14, 15 © Michael S. Yamashita/Corbis; p. 18 © Jack Fields/Corbis; p. 19 © Earl & Nazima Kowall/Corbis; pp. 20–21 © Stephanie Maze/Corbis

Library of Congress Cataloging-in-Publication Data

Fine, Jil.
Writing in ancient China / Jil Fine.
 cm. — (Writing in the ancient world)
Includes bibliographical references and index.
ISBN 0-8239-6510-4 (library binding)
1. Chinese language—Writing—Juvenile literature. I. Title. II. Series.
PL1171 .F56 2003

2002002940

Contents

ANCIENT CHINA

China is the world's oldest living civilization. People have lived in China for more than 250,000 years. No one knows exactly when the Chinese people first started to write.

The oldest samples of ancient Chinese writing are from the people who ruled China from 1900 B.C. to 1300 B.C. This box, used to hold wine, is from that time.

The earliest known pieces of writing in China are from about 3,500 years ago.

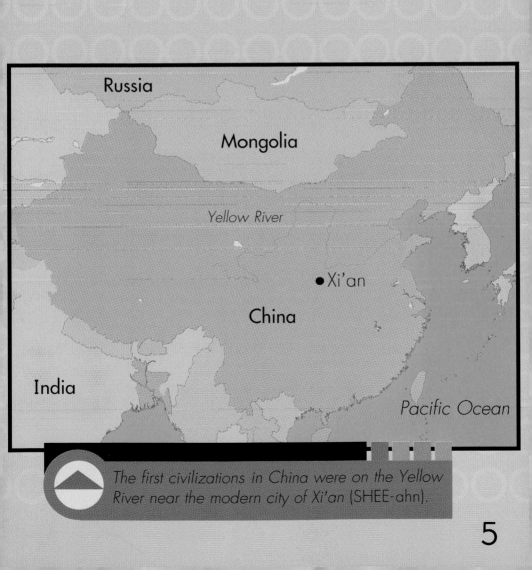

Russia

Mongolia

Yellow River

● Xi'an

China

India

Pacific Ocean

The first civilizations in China were on the Yellow River near the modern city of Xi'an (SHEE-ahn).

EARLY WRITING

The first written records appeared in China around 1766 B.C. At this time, people used a system of writing that had about 3,000 characters. This writing system was much like Chinese writing today.

This bronze figure of a rhinoceros is a bowl with writing on the inside of it (above, right). The ancient Chinese wrote on bones, bronze, stone, and bamboo.

ORACLE BONES

We know a lot about the ancient Chinese because of written records left on oracle bones. Oracle bones were turtle shells or animal bones that had questions about the future carved on them. The ancient Chinese thought that their ancestors could tell them about the future by answering the questions. Each oracle bone had 10 to 60 characters written on it. Over 100,000 oracle bones have been found.

CHECK IT OUT

▶ *In ancient China, most of the questions on the oracle bones were asked by kings. Most of the priests who read the oracle bones were women.*

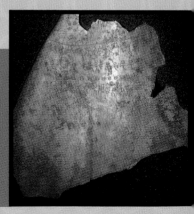

Characters on
an Oracle Bone

Oracle bones were often made from turtle
shells (shown above) or sheep bones.

9

The questions written on oracle bones were usually about family, farming, hunting, or wars. A priest carved a question on a bone. Then, the bone was heated. The heat made the bone crack. The priest studied the cracks to learn the answer to the question. Then, the answer was written on the bone. Later, the priest would also write what actually happened on the bone.

CHECK IT OUT

Oracle bones had a question, the answer to the question, and what really happened. For example, an oracle bone may read: Will the king have a son? (question); Yes (answer); The king had a daughter (what really happened).

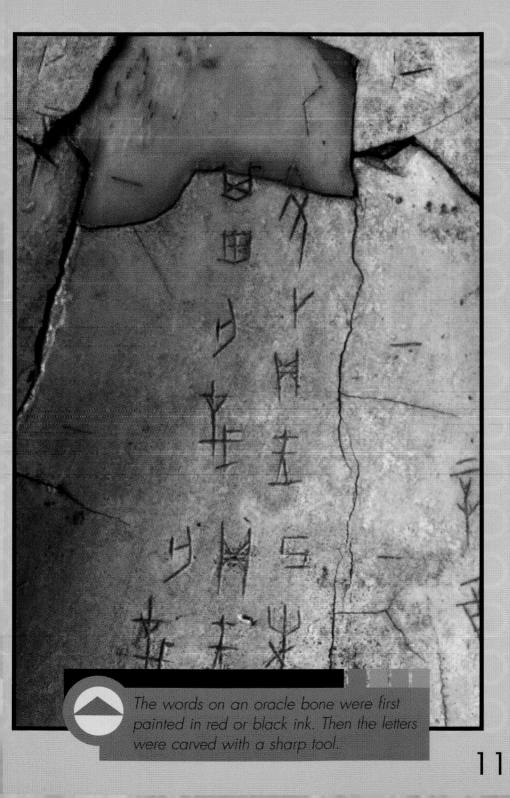

The words on an oracle bone were first painted in red or black ink. Then the letters were carved with a sharp tool.

11

CHINESE WRITING ADVANCES

Starting around 221 B.C., many advances in Chinese writing were made. The writing brush and ink were invented. Ink was made from pine, oil, and other natural materials. Different colors of ink could be made.

People in ancient China burned pine and used the ash to make black ink.

Writing brushes, much like the ones used in ancient China, are still used today.

Writing brushes were made from the hair of animals, such as goats and rabbits. The hair was tied to a piece of wood, bamboo, or clay. At this time many ancient Chinese writings were done on pottery, bamboo, and silk.

There are more than 350 different kinds of bamboo. Most of the ancient Chinese writings on bamboo have not lasted.

Carvings on bamboo from ancient China may have looked something like this.

Important changes to the written language were also made. Early characters looked like the objects for which they stood. About 213 B.C., people started using two characters together to stand for objects or ideas. One character stood for the meaning of the word. The other character stood for the sound of the word.

The Chinese character for autumn is the characters for crops and fire together.

Chinese Writing System

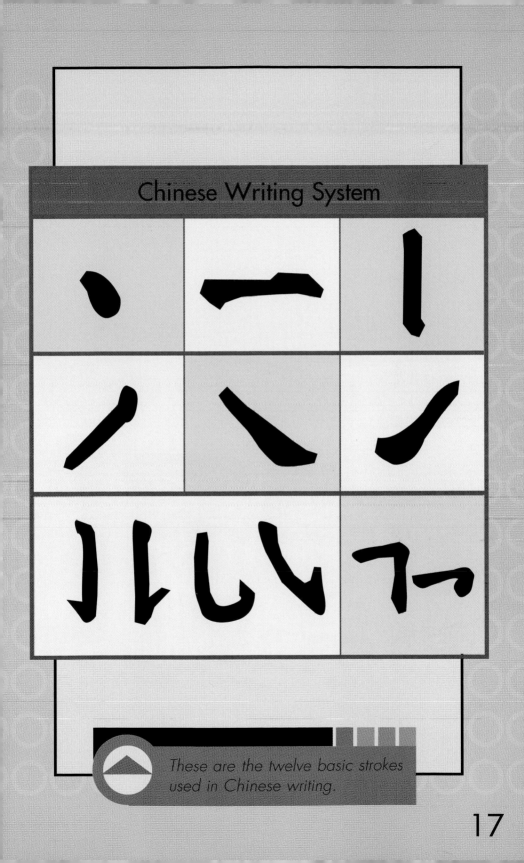

These are the twelve basic strokes used in Chinese writing.

CHINESE WRITING TODAY

In China, people from different areas may not speak the Chinese language the same way. Sometimes, people from different cities or towns cannot understand one another.

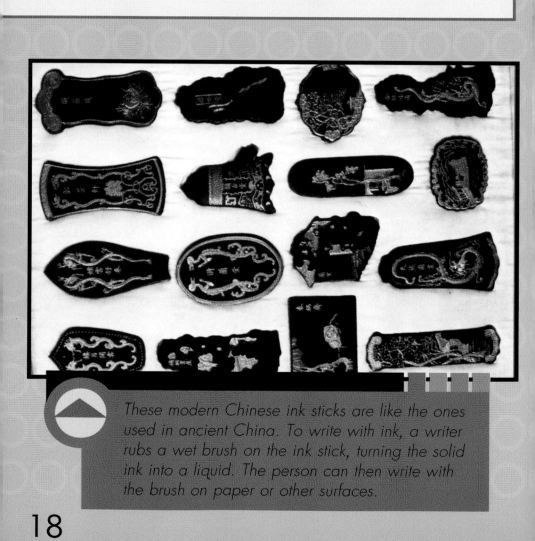

These modern Chinese ink sticks are like the ones used in ancient China. To write with ink, a writer rubs a wet brush on the ink stick, turning the solid ink into a liquid. The person can then write with the brush on paper or other surfaces.

However, most Chinese people can read and understand the written Chinese language. This is because the one character that stands for the meaning of a word is always the same.

In A.D. 105, the Chinese invented paper. They called it bo. The Chinese also invented printing. This man is making paper.

Today, there are about 40,000 different characters in the written Chinese language, but only about 10,000 characters are used. Most of the earliest symbols used by the Chinese can still be read today.

CHECK IT OUT

If you know only 2,000 Chinese characters, you can read most Chinese newspapers.

Written Chinese has changed very little since its ancient beginnings.

Glossary

ancestors (**an**-sehs-tuhrz) family members who have died

bamboo (bam-**boo**) a plant with very tall, stiff, hollow stems

carved (**kahrvd**) to have cut into something with great care

character (**kar**-ihk-tuhr) a mark that stands for something

civilization (sihv-uh-luh-**zay**-shuhn) a way of life that includes cities, written forms of language, and special kinds of work for people

future (**fyoo**-chuhr) the time that is to come; what is going to happen

oracle (**or**-uh-kuhl) someone or something that is believed to be able to tell the future

priests (**preests**) people who are leaders in a church

symbols (**sihm**-buhlz) things that stand for something else

Resources

Books

Ancient China
by Robert Nicholson
Chelsea House Publishing (1995)

Made in China: Ideas and Inventions
from Ancient China
by Suzanne Williams
Pacific View Press (1997)

Web Sites

Due to the changing nature of Internet links, PowerKids
Press has developed an online list of Web sites related
to the subjects of this book. This site is updated regularly.
Please use this link to access the list:

http://www.powerkidslinks.com/waw/anch/

Index

Word Count: 503

Note to Librarians, Teachers, and Parents

    If reading is a challenge, Reading Power is a solution! Reading Power
is perfect for readers who want high-interest subject matter at an accessible reading
level. These fact-filled, photo-illustrated books are designed for readers who want
straightforward vocabulary, engaging topics, and a manageable reading experience.
With clear picture/text correspondence, leveled Reading Power books put the reader
in charge. Now readers have the power to get the information they want and the skills
they need in a user-friendly format.